ORMSBY

TURTLES

By Lois and Louis Darling

WILLIAM MORROW & CO.   NEW YORK, 1962

We wish to thank Dr. Edwin H. Colbert, Chairman of the Department of Paleontology and Curator of Fossil Reptiles and Amphibians, American Museum of Natural History, for his helpful criticism and advice.

11 12 13 14 15

The June woods are almost junglelike with rich green growth. As the sunlight finds its way down through the thick foliage it falls on the banks of a small pool, making golden splotches among the giant leaves of skunk cabbage and the delicate, pointed growth of arrowheads. Downstream it is more open and the banks blend into flat, swampy ground. There rank upon rank of almost impenetrable cattails grow. In the dark waters of the pool columns of sunlight brighten parts of the muddy bottom or fall on water-soaked logs and sunken drifts of last year's leaves. Whirligig beetles and water striders make wavelets and dimples on the surface while dragonflies rustle slightly on stiff transparent wings as they go about their business over the water. Most other living things are quietly resting in the midday warmth. But down deep, in the darkest part of the pool, there is a stir of movement.

Again there is a flick of motion, in a sunny spot
this time, and more definite. Up into the light
swims a huge turtle. Its rough shell looks so much
like the stream bottom or the surface of an old
sunken log that only the slow paddling of web-
footed legs reveals the turtle's presence. It is a big
snapping turtle—a monster of its kind, which would
weigh over thirty pounds and would measure a foot
and a half over the length of its shell.

As the turtle swims nearer the scales on its legs, the sculptured scutes of its shell, and the "saw teeth" on the upper edge of its thick tail become plainly visible. If you do not move at all, the turtle may come closer and closer. In its dark reptilian eyes you imagine you see past ages and you feel that here is an old, old, creature. The soft greenhouse smell of the sun-warmed plants and the brook, the thick green leaves, the rustling dragonflies, and this old reptile may make you feel that time has gone backward and, like a hero in a science-fiction tale, you have been transported into an ancient age—a time when huge dinosaurs roamed the land.

Such a spell of fancy can last only an instant. Off in the distance you may hear the drone of trucks on a modern highway or perhaps the hoot of a railway whistle, and you know that the prehistoric reptile is only a big present-day snapping turtle, not an unusual sight at all.

THE HISTORY OF TURTLES

But in a way such imagining has truth behind it. Turtles are the most ancient type of living reptile. From the evidence of fossils, we know that turtles almost like those that live today inhabited the earth 200 million years ago. Triassochelys was one of these, and although it had a few teeth on its palate and could not retract its head and legs completely inside its shell, as most turtles now can, it was much like its modern relations. Later, 100 million years before human beings first appeared on earth,

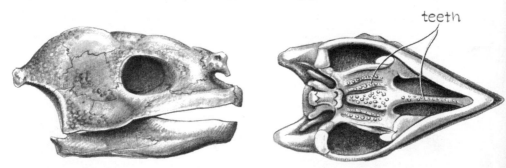

teeth

TRIASSOCHELYS (fossil skull)

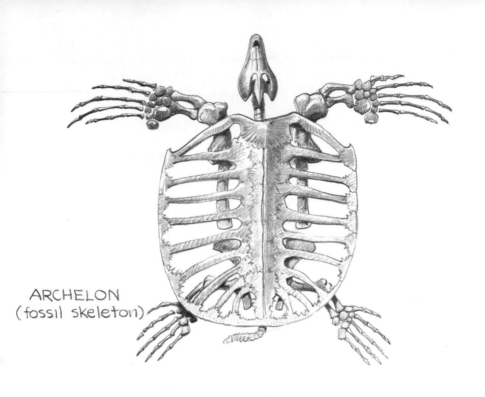

ARCHELON
(fossil skeleton)

such turtles as *Archelon,* twelve feet long and weighing a ton, swam in the seas that covered what is now South Dakota.

In the streams of present-day Brazil there still lives a group of turtles just like those that were living when *Triceratops* and *Tyrannosaurus* disappeared from the earth at the end of the age of dinosaurs. Snapping turtles, very closely related to the one just seen in the brook, lived in Europe during the Miocene epoch, 25 million years ago.

During all these long ages turtles have somehow flourished, regardless of whatever disasters and extinctions overwhelmed so many of their reptile relatives. A famous paleontologist (a scientist who studies ancient life) says, "Because they are still living, turtles are commonplace objects to us. Were they extinct, their shells—the most remarkable defensive armor ever assumed by a tetrapod (four-footed animal)—would be cause for wonder."

All reptiles have descended from certain four-footed, land-living, egg-laying animals, which we know only from their fossil remains. We call these long-extinct reptiles cotylosaurs, or stem reptiles, because they are the ancestors of all other reptiles, living or extinct, and form the "stem" of the reptile family tree.

Cotylosaurs date back to the Carboniferous period, about 250 million years ago. They were somewhat lizardlike in shape, with no very distinctive features. But very slowly, over many, many generations, the descendants of the cotylosaurs began to look very different from their ancestors. In the exciting fossil *Eunotosaurus,* we can see that this cotylosaur descendant had some rather turtlelike characteristics. Although this little animal is hardly what we would call a turtle today, it did have wide, flattened ribs, which, as time went on, might have easily formed the foundation for part of the turtle shell.

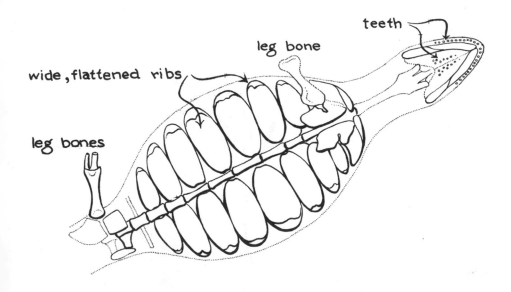

EUNOTOSAURUS lived about 220,000,000 years ago in what we call South Africa.

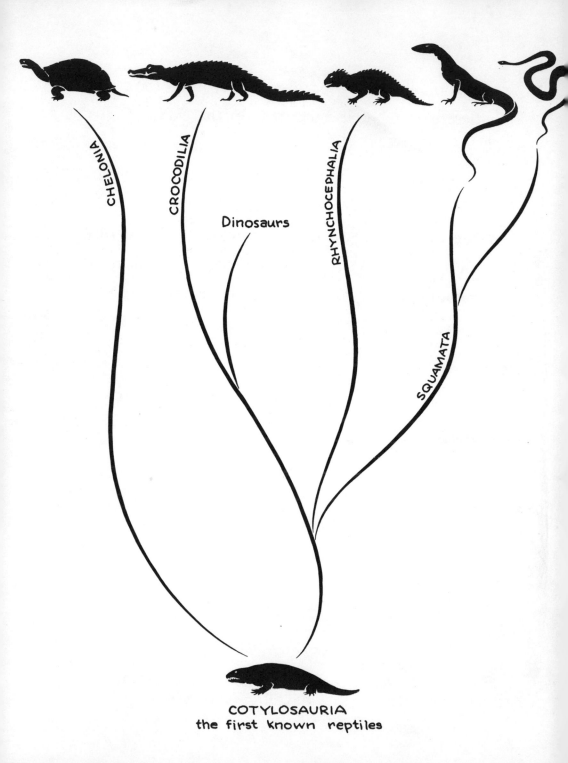

CHELONIA

CROCODILIA

Dinosaurs

RHYNCHOCEPHALIA

SQUAMATA

COTYLOSAURIA
the first known reptiles

Different special features developed in other groups descending from cotylosaurs. As millions of years went by these evolved into the other reptiles we know of today, both living and extinct. From one branch came the birds (class Aves), while from a group of mammal-like reptiles evolved the mammals (class Mammalia).

In spite of having become quite different from other reptiles, turtles still are more like them than any other animal. So science lists, or classifies, them under the class Reptilia, in a smaller grouping called an order—the order Chelonia, from the Greek word for turtle. The other modern orders of the class Reptilia are the order Crocodilia, crocodiles and alligators; the order Rhynchocephalia, the almost extinct tuataras of New Zealand; and the order Squamata, lizards and snakes.

Tuatara

THE STRUCTURE OF TURTLES

The turtle skull has several special features that make it particularly interesting. It has a solid skull roof, which, in a way, is similar to the skulls of the ancient cotylosaurs. This is evidence that turtles are more closely related to the cotylosaurs than to other

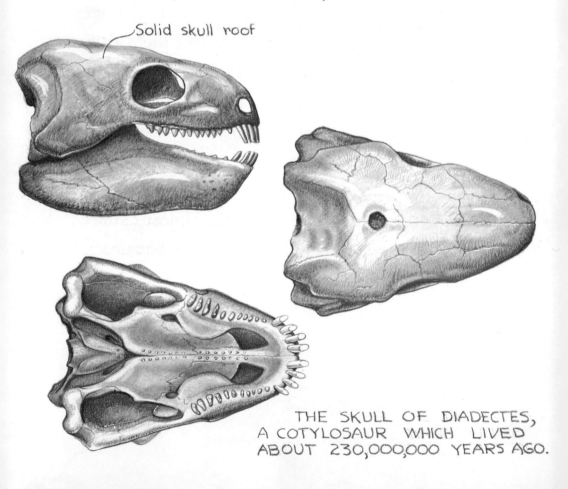

Solid skull roof

THE SKULL OF DIADECTES, A COTYLOSAUR WHICH LIVED ABOUT 230,000,000 YEARS AGO.

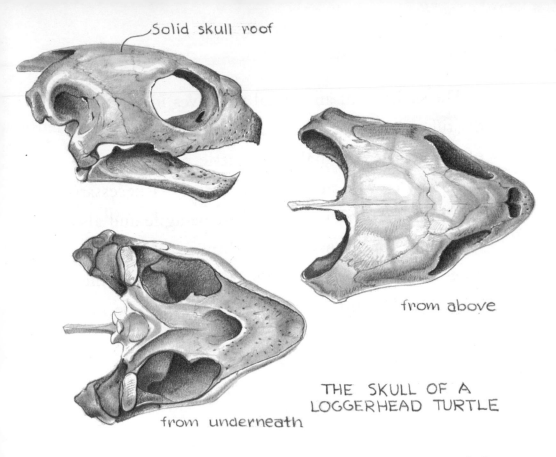

Solid skull roof

from above

THE SKULL OF A
LOGGERHEAD TURTLE

from underneath

reptiles, and it helps prove that they have descended directly from these ancestors of millions of years ago.

In place of teeth the horny covering of the beak is very sharp along the edges and serves to catch and hold food as well as to slice it into pieces small enough to swallow—the only chewing a turtle ever does.

The skeleton of an animal that lives inside a box of stiff armor is, of course, quite different from that of an ordinary animal. The turtle neck vertebrae have very complicated flexible joints—a necessary condition for a neck which must be agile and also be able to fold compactly within a shell. On the other hand, many of the turtle back vertebrae, which have flexible joints in most animals, have become

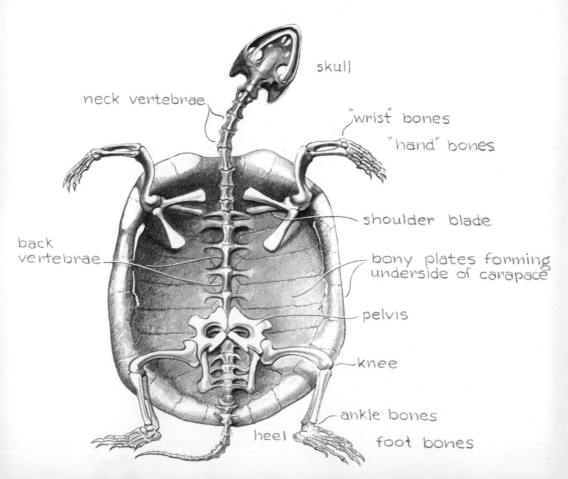

skull

neck vertebrae

"wrist" bones

"hand" bones

shoulder blade

back
vertebrae

bony plates forming
underside of carapace

pelvis

knee

ankle bones

heel

foot bones

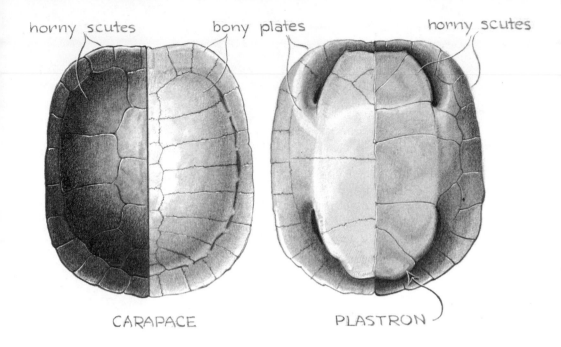

horny scutes   bony plates   horny scutes

CARAPACE   PLASTRON

fused to the bony plates of the shell. Other back vertebrae, which existed in turtle ancestors, disappeared when the turtle body became shorter and shorter as its shell evolved.

As everyone knows, this shell makes the turtle among the most completely armored of all living things. The solid part of the armor is composed of an upper shell (carapace) and a lower shell (plastron). Outermost on the shells are the horny scutes, which developed from ancestral scales. The scutes are supported underneath by strong bony plates.

Some species, such as box turtles, are better protected by their shells than are others, like the snapping turtle. Box turtles have a large domed carapace. The plastron has two parts, joined by a hinge, which form "trap doors." When the head, legs, and tail are drawn in between the shells, these hinged sections of the plastron close the openings so tightly that it is almost impossible for a predator,

hinge

EASTERN BOX TURTLE

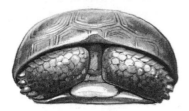

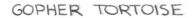

looking for a meal of turtle, to break through.

The turtles of the tortoise family have another means of completely protecting themselves. When their heads are withdrawn, they close the opening with their legs, which are covered with very hard and sometimes bony scales. These armored legs offer as much resistance to predators as does the box turtle's hinged plastron.

Turtles like the snapping turtle, for instance, are not so well protected by their shell. The snapper's head, tail, and legs are so bulky and its shell so comparatively small that it does not completely protect the soft parts. But snappers more than make up for this seeming weakness with their powerful sharp-edged jaws, their ability to strike with lightning speed, and their absolute lack of fear of any living thing when they are cornered.

Turtle ears have no outside parts that can be seen, as yours do. But the hearing equipment in their skulls is much like yours, complete with eardrums,

DIAGRAM OF A
TURTLE EAR

Stapes bone ⎫ columella
Cartilage ⎭

Nerves of balance
and of hearing

Eardrum (skin is not
very different from that
on other parts of head).

which vibrate when sound waves strike them. The tiny columella, consisting of a cartilage and the small stapes bone, then carries the vibrations from the eardrum to the inner ear, where the vibrations are changed to messages sent to the brain over the nerves of hearing.

A few species of turtles can grunt and others squeak occasionally. They make these noises by quickly exhaling their breath or by rubbing their jaws together. As turtles have no vocal cords, they cannot be said to have a real voice. The well-known Bible phrase, "The voice of the turtle is heard in our land," was probably a mistake in translation and may originally have meant the voice of the turtle dove.

THE LIFE OF TURTLES

There are about 200 different species of turtles alive today. They have a wide range of size and shape, and are adapted to many different ways of living. For instance, the small bog turtle averages only three inches in shell length while the Galápagos tortoise is a huge animal, which may weigh as much as 400 pounds. Such land turtles as these walk about on clublike, elephantine feet while most water turtles have flattened feet with webbed toes. The great sea turtles all have their feet modified into large swimming flippers. Some turtles have

BOG TURTLE

GALÁPAGOS TORTOISE

HAWKSBILL TURTLE

BOX TURTLE

SNAPPING TURTLE

SOFT-SHELLED TURTLE

hard, heavy shells, which may encase their entire body. Others have only partial shells, while still others, like the soft-shelled turtles, have even lost the hard turtle armor and are so flat that they are called flapjack turtles.

Turtles live over a great part of the world. In temperate and tropical climates almost every body of fresh water has a population of at least a few of the multitude of fresh-water species. Many deserts are inhabited by land-living tortoises, and the sea turtles range the open oceans.

Unlike birds and mammals, reptiles have little control over the temperature of their bodies. Their temperature varies with the temperature of their surroundings. Reptiles become sluggish when it is cold and quickly freeze to death if the temperature drops low enough. So turtles must bury themselves in earth or in the mud of stream bottoms in climates where there are cold winters. In warmer climates turtles are active all year round.

Also, because they have no control over their inside temperature, turtles will quickly die from overheating if they are exposed to the hot sun for too long. Turtles that live in very warm places, like deserts, often are active only during the cool part of the day, and bury themselves or find shade when the sun is strongest.

COMMON SNAPPING TURTLE

The common snapping turtle is a member of the family Chelydridae, and is one of the most widespread species in North America. It ranges all over the eastern half of the United States and the southern part of Canada. It lives in almost all kinds of fresh-water habitats and even in brackish pools in some places.

Snapping turtles will eat almost anything they can find or capture, dead or alive. They eat some fishes, including those valuable to man, animals such as salamanders and frogs, and much plant food. Snappers have also been known to kill young ducklings. Because of these habits, in addition to what most people think of as an ugly appearance, a disagreeable disposition, and their well-known ability to defend themselves, snappers have had a bad reputation. However, careful studies of them have made us change our minds a bit. Actual figures show that

the supposed damage they do does not really amount to much and a snapper will not bother a human being who does not bother it first. Can an animal be thought disagreeable and vicious because it is well able to defend itself and catch its food efficiently? If snapping turtles could feel and think like human beings, they would consider themselves merely strong and courageous. When you get to know and understand these reptiles as they go about the daily business of living, you may come to think of them as rather beautiful.

On almost any day in June a female snapper may haul herself out of the water to find a dry-land location, where she will dig her nest and lay her eggs. She will have mated with a male snapper some time before, perhaps a very long time before. Female snappers often travel a considerable distance from water to find a suitable spot in which to dig a nest. A proper egg-laying location has mysterious qualities known only to turtles, for they often pass by spots which would seem ideal for the purpose to us.

They always make their nests in quite open places, with plenty of sunlight to warm and hatch the eggs. They also seem to prefer places where it is easy to dig, and they are sometimes seen laying their eggs on dirt roads and at the edges of plowed fields.

When the female snapper finds an egg-laying spot to suit her, she slowly begins to work with her strong clawed hind feet. By pushing backward, first with one foot and then the other, the turtle patiently scrapes until a hole six or seven inches deep has been dug. Then the round white eggs are laid rapidly. There may be anywhere from a dozen to fifty or more eggs in a snapper's nest.

As the eggs are laid the mother turtle arranges them in the nest with her hind feet. When the laying is completed she fills up the hole, working and packing the earth back again. She never once turns around to look at the eggs or nest. When it is completely covered, packed to the right degree, and smoothed over, so as to attract as little notice as possible from the hungry world, the job of reproduction is over as far as the female turtle is concerned. Time, sun, fate, and the age-old miracle of developing life will decide the future of the small turtles to be. Their mother is soon back in the brook, feeding and basking. She will never knowingly see her offspring.

We all know that birds' eggs will not develop until the parent bird warms them with the heat of its body by brooding them or until they are warmed in an incubator. Because of this even, dependable heat, the new bird forming inside the egg grows quickly and at a steady pace. Each species of bird has its own special time for hatching. A mallard duckling, for instance, hatches in twenty-eight to thirty days, and a young chicken in about twenty-one days. So, once brooding has begun, it is easy to predict when a baby bird will hatch.

Reptiles do not brood their eggs. It would be quite useless if they did, of course, because their bodies are little, if any, warmer than the temperature of the surroundings. So turtle eggs must depend entirely upon the heat of the sun to develop. The eggs of many species may hatch in three months or so, if the weather is favorable. But if the season is cool and rainy and the eggs were laid late, they may not hatch at all during that summer. In this case, if

they happen to be buried deep enough to escape frost, the eggs will hatch the following spring, when the suns warms the earth again.

Baby turtles break out of their shell after hundreds of quick tapping movements with the sharp egg tooth on the tip of their beaks. Egg teeth are common to both baby birds and reptiles and drop off after hatching. When free of the shell the little turtles must struggle up through the hard-packed earth with what must be a mighty effort for such small animals. After resting a bit they make their way slowly to the nearest water, keeping well hidden.

Hatching is a dangerous time for turtles, perhaps the most dangerous of their entire lives. There is no animal but man that is much of a threat to a full-grown snapper and, because of their armor, most other adult turtles are almost free from fear of predators. But little hatchlings, with shells still soft and jaws too tiny to bite, make easy prey. Skunks, weasels, foxes, dogs, rats, snakes, crows, hawks, and—in the water—large turtles and fish, all like tender young turtle.

Hatchling turtles seem to know which way the nearest water lies, although they are often not able to see it when they come out of the shell. It is

thought that they are born with the unlearned instinct of traveling in a downhill direction, or of always heading toward an area of open sky, or both. Thus they almost always end up in watery surroundings. However they do it, they manage to accomplish this remarkable feat without the slightest chance of being taught by their elders or of learning from experience. There is no need to learn in this case. The ability is inherited, just as much as is the shape of their beak or the color of their shell. When they have reached the water the young turtles are able to hide so well that they are seldom seen until they are several years older.

A few years ago we built a house near the stream described at the beginning. During the building the ground was torn up, and there was much bare loosened earth. That spring the snappers swarmed out of the brook to take advantage of the easy digging in loose earth and to lay their eggs all around our new house. Unfortunately we were much too busy to mark and protect any of the nests with wire covering so that we would know when the baby turtles hatched. From the evidence of dug-out nests and curled scraps of leathery reptile eggshell, we knew that skunks had found most of the nests. Turtle eggs are a favorite skunk food, and these animals are very skillful at finding the buried, hidden nests. This is a good thing, too. If skunks, as well as other animals, did not eat many of the snapper eggs, brooks and ponds would soon become crowded with hungry turtles. Places where snapping turtles do become a real menace to the wildlife are often the ones where skunks have been eliminated.

The mud and musk turtles of the family Kinosternidae, a few species of which are shown here, are fresh-water turtles. But the vast majority of fresh-water turtles belong to the large family Emydidae.

The spotted turtle is a member of this family. This pretty reptile lives in the smaller bodies of water—ponds, swampy ditches, woodland pools, bogs, and the like. It is fairly common from south-

Double hinges

Triangular scute - Plastron large

EASTERN

A MUD TURTLE

Single hinge

Squarish scute - Plastron small

STINKPOT

A MUSK TURTLE

SPOTTED TURTLE

eastern Canada to Georgia and west to Illinois.
Spotted turtles are up and about early in the spring
—April in southern New England—when they are
coming out of winter hibernation and looking for
mates. When the spotted turtles can be seen in
marshy ponds and the nights are shrill with the call
of that tiny frog, the spring peeper, you can really
feel that winter is over and that a long, lovely summer lies ahead.

A well-known species of the family Emydidae
is the famous diamondback terrapin, which may
have had a very narrow escape from extinction. This
turtle lives in salt marshes, creeks, and shallow, protected bays containing salt or brackish water. There
is no record of a diamondback inhabiting fresh
water. Otherwise, they are much like many other
fresh-water species of the family Emydidae. Their
one outstanding difference, the taste of their meat,
was almost their undoing. Although they have been
eaten since colonial times, when they were aston-
ishingly plentiful, diamondback terrapin did not

become dangerously popular for food until 1890 or thereabouts. From the glittering Gay Nineties until just after the First World War, terrapin were popular among wealthy and fashionable people out of all possible proportion to their tastiness. One was considered a mere nothing in the world of high society if one didn't eat terrapin regularly.

But there weren't enough terrapins to go around, and they became scarcer and scarcer and more and more expensive. By 1920 owners of marshes were paid $90 a dozen for diamondbacks collected on their property. The turtles had become so scarce and valuable that the United States Bureau of Fisheries experimented in raising them in captivity and a few turtle farms were started. People even tried releasing them in waters far away from their natural range in such places as California and Italy. But diamondbacks were never able to thrive in any but their native regions.

The consumption of diamondback terrapin became such a fad that, like all fads, it did not last.

Although the latest edition of the famous *Fanny Farmer Cookbook* contains two recipes for cooking terrapin and although their meat may be bought canned, not many diamondbacks are eaten today. Many of those that are marketed are raised in captivity. This sharp drop in popularity, plus protective laws in some states, has allowed this persecuted species to recover slowly from dangerously small numbers. Diamondbacks are becoming more and more plentiful each year, although their numbers will never again even approach those that existed in the fertile salt marshes of the past, because we are fast losing these useful and beautiful wet lands forever.

Although almost all turtles of the family Emydidae are aquatic, or water-dwelling, one group in the family is decidedly land-living. These are the box turtles. They range all through eastern and central United States and into Mexico.

Box turtles live in open, moist woodland. While they do not live in the water, they like to have a good deal of it handy for drinking and for an occasional bath, which they appear to enjoy immensely. Each box turtle stays quite faithfully within its own rather small territory of a few acres at most. When you become well acquainted with the habits of an individual turtle, you can generally manage to meet it somewhere in its usual haunts whenever you want to.

Box turtles are omnivorous and eat almost anything—slugs, snails, earthworms, insects, both larval and adult, and much plant life. They are particularly fond of mushrooms and fruit, and will gorge on wild strawberries in season.

These gentle turtles are easy to keep in captivity. Consequently they have been closely observed and their habits and ages well recorded. Careful examinations of box-turtle records by scientists have led to the conclusion that box turtles have lived from eighty to one hundred and twenty-three years and easily average forty to fifty years. While these figures do not match the turtle's legendary reputation for long life, they do represent ripe old ages for such small animals. So it seems that this reputation is well deserved.

One feature of turtle behavior is a fine example of how those inherited traits we call instincts come about. Box turtles can deal safely with rough ground and high places. When placed on a high table or bench, a box turtle will cautiously approach the edge and walk along it, but almost never tumble over. This is because box turtles have been evolving for millions of years as land animals and living on uneven ground where a fall could be a dangerous

accident. During all this time those turtles with this trait were better able to get along, for it helped them to live on land a little more successfully than the other members of their species. More survived to produce offspring. Those offspring that inherited the trait also survived better and produced offspring of their own, and so on. In this way box-turtle behavior, along with such physical characteristics as the shape of the shell, has very slowly become more and more suitable for a land-living life.

This does not seem like a very important observation until we contrast the traits of the box turtle with the traits of water turtles, which have evolved for a life in and around water. They seldom encounter high places and are in no danger when they do, because water turtles almost always land in water when they slither or fall from steep banks, logs, or rocks. The inheritance of an instinctive fear of high places was of no advantage to water turtles, so it never became common among them. Therefore, when they are placed on a table they will plunge over the edge, no matter how high it may be.

Such instinctive behavior controls most of the activity of the so-called lower animals like reptiles, birds, and insects, to name a few. It works very well when the animals in question are leading normal lives in the kind of surroundings in which their species evolved. The box turtle seldom falls from a high place, and the water turtle does not hurt itself when it falls into water. But when people take animals out of their normal surroundings, as was done when the turtles were put on the table, the true nature of their actions, which ordinarily seem intelligent, is often shown to be unreasoning, fixed instinct. Then we are tempted to think of the animals as stupid. Turtles cannot be called stupid, however, because they have lived successfully in their varied natural habitats for millions and millions of years.

In North America there are only three species of the turtle family Testudinidae, or the land-tortoise family. These are the gopher tortoises. One species is called, naturally enough, the gopher tortoise. It ranges from South Carolina to the tip of Florida and westward to Texas. The other two species are Berlander's tortoise and the desert tortoise, which live in the far west.

DESERT TORTOISE

GOPHER TORTOISE

    Gopher tortoises are expert diggers. They make large burrows from ten to thirty-five feet long, which are, more or less, their permanent homes. These burrows are also used by a variety of other animals such as diamondback rattlesnakes, frogs, possums, and raccoons.

    Like all tortoises, gopher tortoises have what can only be described as elephantlike legs. The front legs, though, are somewhat flattened, an adaptation that makes digging easier. Tortoise toes are not webbed.

Perhaps the most famous tortoises in the world are the huge tortoises of the Galápagos Islands. Here on the equator, about 600 miles off the west coast of South America, live animals and plants that, while closely related to South American species, are found nowhere else on earth but on these lonely islands. So the Galápagos are like a little world in themselves, and are a wonderful natural laboratory in which to study the slow changes, or evolution, which take place in all living things.

It was the giant tortoises, the birds, lizards, and other animals of the Galápagos that helped young Charles Darwin form his world-shaking ideas about evolution. He visited the islands in 1835 during his five-year cruise around the world as naturalist on the British exploring vessel HMS *Beagle.* In his account of the famous trip, popularly known as *The Voyage of the Beagle,* he describes the habits of the tortoises and tells how he rode on their backs. Of this he says, "I frequently got on their backs, and

then giving a few raps on the hinder part of their shells, they would rise up and walk away;—but I found it very difficult to keep my balance."

The story of these huge harmless reptiles is one of the many sad ones in the history of man's association with the other animals that share the world with him. Fresh meat was a scarce and welcome article on ships at sea in the days before refrigeration. The Galápagos tortoises were easily caught, and provided large quantities of fresh meat, which could be kept almost indefinitely by the simple means of caging the turtles alive on shipboard until the crew was ready to use them. In this way the sailor's hard

life was made more pleasant and his diet more healthy. But as many as 350 tortoises were often captured by a single ship. It has been calculated, from records in old ships' logbooks, that 10,000 tortoises were taken from the Galápagos by American whale ships alone between 1831 and 1865.

Colonists on the islands also used the tortoises for food without any attempt to understand their ways or to conserve them. In addition to this, pigs, dogs, cats, and rats were brought by men to the islands. These animals made tortoise reproduction, slow at best, almost impossible, for they preyed on eggs and baby tortoises. So a species of animal that could have been a lasting food resource and a source of enjoyment and wonder, if used wisely, is now a pitiful remnant threatened with extinction.

The great sea turtles are the most completely adapted to water life of all the turtles. They spend almost their whole time in the ocean except for a few hours when the females come to the beaches to lay their eggs. The sea turtles are classified under two families, the leatherback sea turtles and the true sea turtles.

There is only one species of leatherback turtle. This largest of living turtles may grow to be 7 feet

long and weigh 1200 pounds. It is possible that the biggest leatherbacks reach a ton in weight, although there is no official record of such a monster turtle. Leatherback turtles have no horny shell covering and only a comparatively few irregular plates. In such large turtles a regular shell would be tremendously heavy. Loss of the heavy shell is doubtless an advantage that helped produce a more bouyant swimming animal.

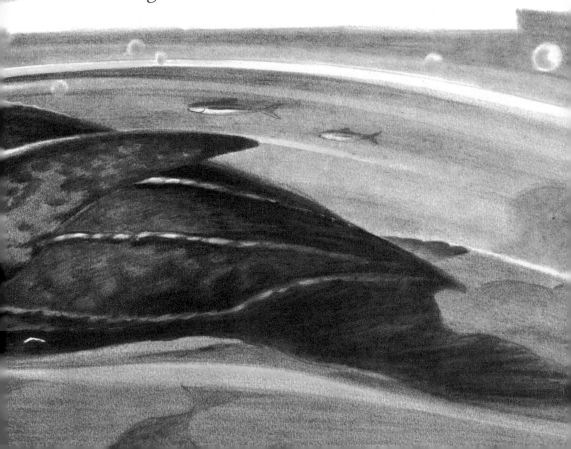

The true sea turtles are smaller than leatherbacks, and all have regular turtle shells. They are the green turtle, the loggerhead, the olive-backed, the hawksbill turtles, and the ridley.

Some of these turtles have also been recklessly wasted by man. Before the days of plastics the hawksbill turtles were immensely valuable for the beautiful and useful objects of tortoise shell that were made from their shells. The green turtle is perhaps still the most valuable in the world for food as it is much in demand for the famous turtle soup. Green turtles are not only caught and eaten in every possible way and place, but their eggs are gathered from beaches throughout their range. From one small South Pacific island 1,790,370 green-turtle eggs were taken from the beaches in one year. It is easy to see that in spite of the fertility of these great sea reptiles, their numbers are steadily growing less from year to year.

TURTLE KEEPING

A female spotted turtle dug its nest in a neighbor's petunia bed several years ago. Our friend was not interested in raising turtles, so we moved the eggs to our own garden to save them from the effects of weeding, transplanting, and insect sprays. We carefully "planted" the four white eggs at exactly the same depth and in about the same degree of daily sunshine as that in which the mother turtle had laid them in the first place. Over the spot we fitted a small wire cage to protect the eggs and to hold the small turtles when they hatched.

One day in late August there were four small yellow spotted turtles, less than the size of quarters, under the wire cage. We watched while three of the hatchlings hurried away toward a nearby pond, making great work of scrambling over or under every twig, stone, or lump of dirt. The fourth turtle we kept. It lived, under the name of Turtox, in a small

terrarium on our kitchen window sill for several years. Finally Turtox got too large and active to be comfortable in so small a space. Then we took him back to the nearby pond that his brothers and sisters had headed for so long ago and watched him swim away, down into the weedy depths.

Turtles are interesting to keep in captivity and are valuable for scientific study. Most pet-store turtles are the young of southern species, such as the red-eared turtle. Many other turtles are also fairly easy to keep. Observation of their habits in terrariums and aquariums helps us to understand them in the wild. Since surprisingly little is known about the habits of many species, any naturalist, young or old, can make a useful contribution to science by recording careful, accurate observations of many of our common turtles in their natural surroundings.

When kept in captivity, turtles should always be provided with conditions that match as closely as possible those in which they would live naturally. It is important to give them the right amount of light, temperature, and moisture. Their food should also be similar to what they would find in the wild. Of course, determining such a diet is hard, because so little is known about the food of many species. But most turtles will eat vegetables like lettuce;

such fruits as bananas, apples, strawberries, and melons; lean meat; earthworms (either whole or cut into small pieces, depending on the size of the turtle or the worm); meal worms and other insects; and bits of fish and shellfish. If you cannot feed your turtle fish, add a bit of bone meal to the meat you use. So-called "turtle food" is not generally satisfactory as a steady diet, although a great variety of healthy foods can be purchased from reliable aquarium companies and pet stores. A drop or two of cod-liver oil added to chopped lean meat and fed now and then will help insure the proper vitamins. A lump of plaster of Paris kept in the aquarium water will help to supply the calcium needed for strong bones, including the bony part of the shell. At any rate, turtle diets, like those of many animals, should be varied.

Many water turtles will eat only under water, and so must be fed where the water is deep enough for them to submerge. Always remember to clean out scraps of leftover food after feeding, so that they will not pollute the water. Or, better yet, train your turtles to eat their meals in a separate feeding tank or large bowl, which can be easily washed afterward. Remember also that turtles are reptiles and are sluggish, when compared to birds or to mammals like your dog or yourself. They do not eat often and do not eat much. Three times a week may be enough. Try to feed a turtle no more than it will eat in a short time.

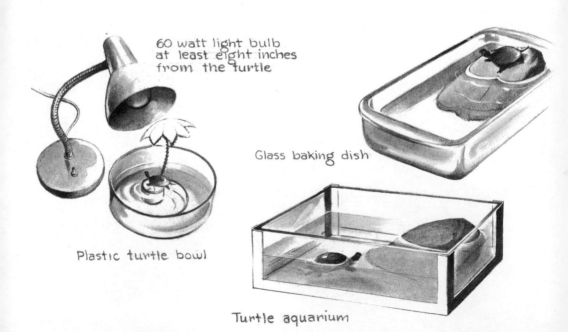

60 watt light bulb at least eight inches from the turtle

Glass baking dish

Plastic turtle bowl

Turtle aquarium

Handle turtles only when necessary. It is almost as easy to kill a captive animal with too much mistaken kindness as it is to kill it with cruelty or neglect. Warmth may be provided by an electric light bulb. Forty to sixty watts is about the right strength, but care should be taken not to overheat the turtle by placing the bulb too close to it. Also turtles are easily chilled. The tap water in your aquarium should be heated to 75 degrees Fahrenheit, and the container should never be placed on a window sill that is cold and drafty. If sunlight is not available in a draft-free spot, you may use an electric lamp as a substitute sun for many species.

Turtles need a dry place to crawl out on and a certain amount of sunlight is helpful in preventing fatal disease. However, too much sun for too long, particularly that shining through a glass window, can overheat and kill them. It is best to make sure that some shade is always available. Then the turtle can itself regulate the amount of sunlight it needs.

Actually turtles are not of any great value when compared to such domestic animals as chickens or cows. When we fear for the future of such animals as the Galápagos tortoises, many people say, "Why worry? What good are turtles?"

Judged by a standard of dollars, turtles are really not much good. But to ask, "What good are turtles?" does not really mean a thing. We might as well ask, "What good are you?" Both ourselves and turtles are marvelous and beautiful creatures of nature. The gentle box turtle wandering in its patch of woodland, the great green turtle hauling itself out of the surf to lay its eggs on the moonlit beach of some tropic isle, the old snapper in the muddy pool, which reminds you so much of ancient times and creatures—all these, along with you and countless other animals and plants, are products of more than 2000 million years of changing life on earth. Each species is an irreplaceable part of the miracle of life.